A to Z

CHRISTIAN LIBRARY

ANO

MW00812836

Praise and Wo... ...es

40 Piano Arrangements of Contemporary Christian Favorites

Arranged by Carol Tornquist

Alfred

Produced by
Alfred Music
P.O. Box 10003
Van Nuys, CA 91410-0003
alfred.com

ISBN-10: 1-4706-2354-4
ISBN-13: 978-1-4706-2354-8

Cover Photos:
Woman and birds: © Gettyimages.com / ipopba • Abstract swirl background: Gettyimages.com / ChrisGorgio

Contents

Amazing Grace (My Chains Are Gone) 4

Amazing Love (My Lord, What Love Is This) 6

Be the Centre 9

Beautiful Things 12

Cornerstone 20

Days of Elijah 15

Everlasting God 24

Forever 30

Forever Reign 27

Glorious Day (Living He Loved Me) 34

God of Wonders 38

Hallelujah (Your Love Is Amazing) 41

Holy Is the Lord 44

Holy Spirit, Rain Down 48

How Great Is Our God 51

How He Loves 54

I Can Only Imagine 58

I Could Sing of Your Love Forever 62

I Lift My Eyes Up 65

In Christ Alone (My Hope Is Found) 72

Indescribable 68

Jesus, Draw Me Ever Nearer 75

King of Heaven 78

Let It Rise 84

Lord, Reign in Me 81

Mighty to Save 88

No Other Name 92

Oceans (Where Feet May Fail) 94

One Thing Remains (Your Love Never Fails) 97

Open the Eyes of My Heart 100

Our God 104

The Power of the Cross (Oh, to See the Dawn) 107

Revelation Song 110

There Is a Redeemer 114

There Is None Like You 117

This Is Amazing Grace 120

Untitled Hymn (Come to Jesus) 123

Victor's Crown 134

We Believe 126

Your Grace Is Enough 130

(Approx. Performance Time – 2:00)

Amazing Grace
(My Chains Are Gone)

Words and Music by
Chris Tomlin and Louie Giglio
Arr. Carol Tornquist

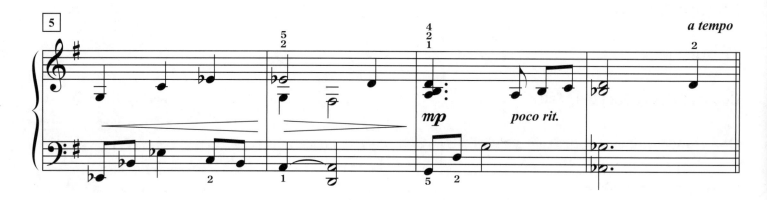

(Approx. Performance Time – 2:45)

Amazing Love
(My Lord, What Love Is This)

Words and Music by Graham Kendrick
Arr. Carol Tornquist

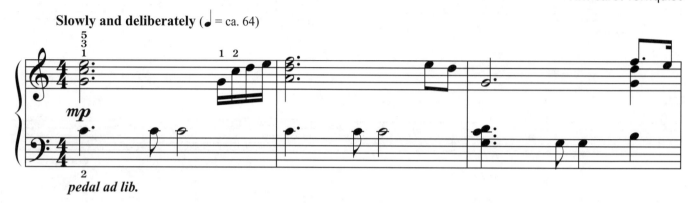

(Approx. Performance Time – 2:30)

Be the Centre

Words and Music by Michael Frye
Arr. Carol Tornquist

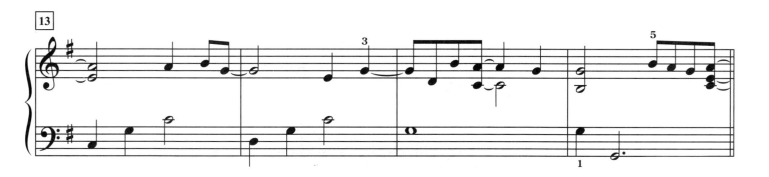

(Approx. Performance Time – 2:30)

Beautiful Things

Words and Music by
Lisa Gungor and Michael Gungor
Arr. Carol Tornquist

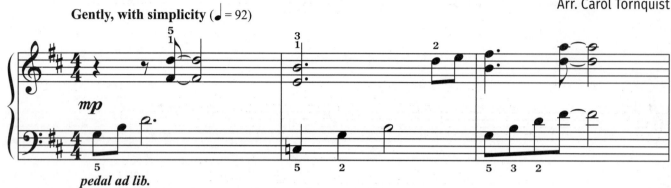

(Approx. Performance Time – 3:15)

Days of Elijah

Words and Music by Robin Mark
Arr. Carol Tornquist

(Approx. Performance Time – 3:15)

Cornerstone

Words and Music by Edward Mote,
Eric Liljero, Jonas Myrin and Reuben Morgan
Arr. Carol Tornquist

(Approx. Performance Time – 1:45)

Everlasting God

Words and Music by
Brenton Brown and Ken Riley
Arr. Carol Tornquist

(Approx. Performance Time – 2:00)

Forever Reign

Words and Music by
Jason Ingram and Reuben Morgan
Arr. Carol Tornquist

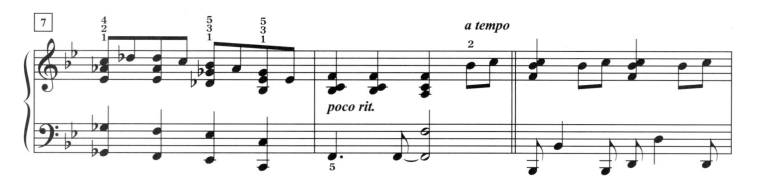

(Approx. Performance Time – 3:15)

Forever

Words and Music by Brian Johnson, Christa Black Gifford,
Gabe Wilson, Jenn Johnson, Joel Taylor and Kari Jobe

Arr. Carol Tornquist

(Approx. Performance Time – 3:00)

Glorious Day
(Living He Loved Me)

Words and Music by
Mark Hall and Michael Bleecker
Arr. Carol Tornquist

Steady four ($\quad$ = 88)

(Approx. Performance Time – 2:45)

God of Wonders

Words and Music by
Marc Byrd and Steve Hindalong
Arr. Carol Tornquist

(Approx. Performance Time – 2:15)

Hallelujah
(Your Love Is Amazing)

Words and Music by
Brenton Brown and Brian Doerksen
Arr. Carol Tornquist

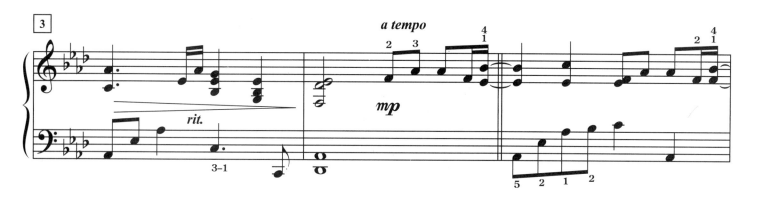

(Approx. Performance Time – 3:15)

Holy Is the Lord

Words and Music by
Chris Tomlin and Louie Giglio
Arr. Carol Tornquist

(Approx. Performance Time – 2:15)

Holy Spirit, Rain Down

Words and Music by Russell Fragar
Arr. Carol Tornquist

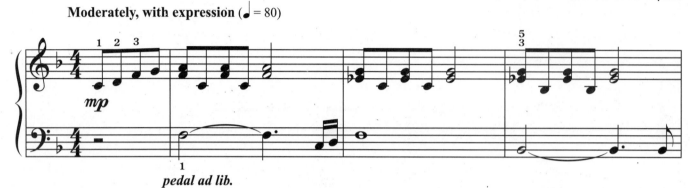

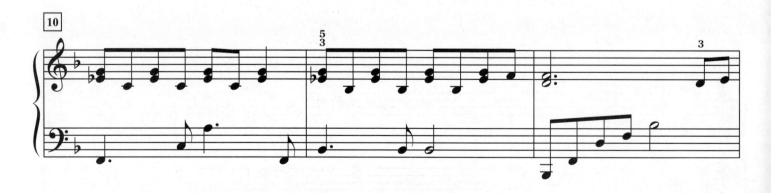

(Approx. Performance Time – 2:15)

How Great Is Our God

Words and Music by
Jesse Reeves, Chris Tomlin and Ed Cash
Arr. Carol Tornquist

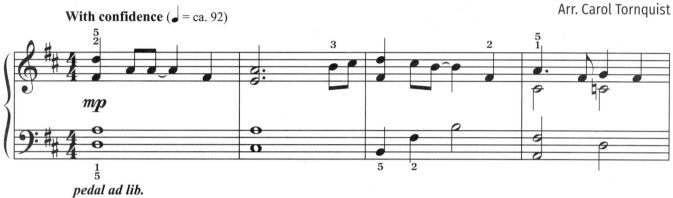

(Approx. Performance Time – 3:00)

How He Loves

Words and Music by John Mark McMillan
Arr. Carol Tornquist

(Approx. Performance Time – 3:15)

I Can Only Imagine

Words and Music by Bart Millard
Arr. Carol Tornquist

(Approx. Performance Time – 2:00)

I Could Sing of Your Love Forever

Words and Music by Martin Smith
Arr. Carol Tornquist

(Approx. Performance Time – 2:15)

I Lift My Eyes Up
(Psalm 121)

Words and Music by Brian Doerksen
Arr. Carol Tornquist

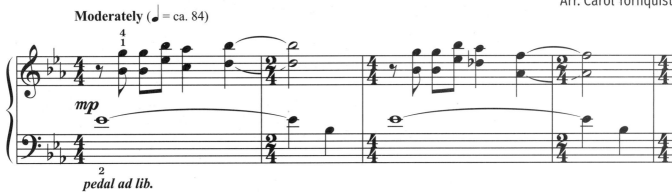

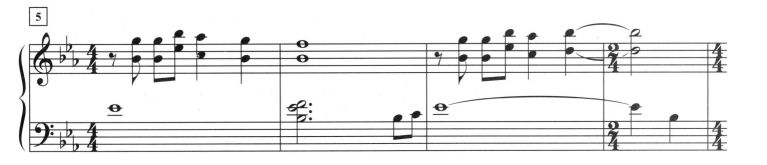

(Approx. Performance Time – 2:30)

Indescribable

Words and Music by
Jesse Reeves and Laura Story
Arr. Carol Tornquist

(Approx. Performance Time – 2:00)

In Christ Alone
(My Hope Is Found)

Words and Music by
Stuart Townend and Keith Getty
Arr. Carol Tornquist

Not hurried, with rubato (♩ = ca. 72)

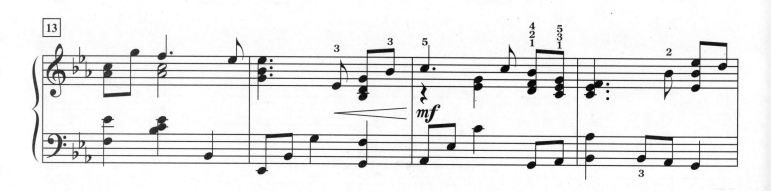

(Approx. Performance Time – 2:30)

Jesus, Draw Me Ever Nearer

Words and Music by
Keith Getty and Margaret Becker
Arr. Carol Tornquist

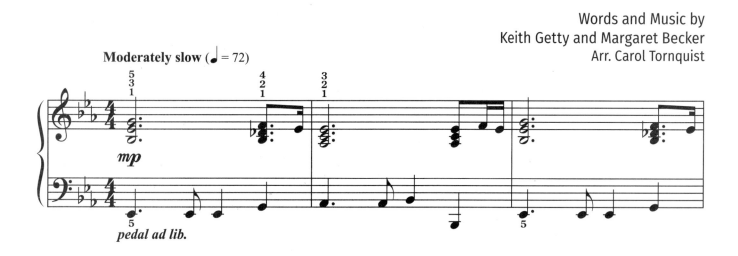

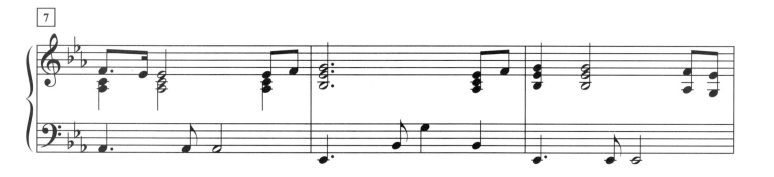

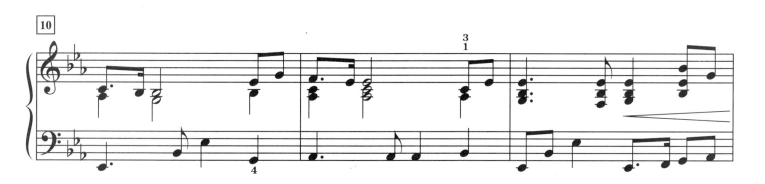

King of Heaven

Words and Music by
Jason Ingram and Paul Baloche
Arr. Carol Tornquist

(Approx. Performance Time – 1:45)

Lord, Reign in Me

Words and Music by Brenton Brown
Arr. Carol Tornquist

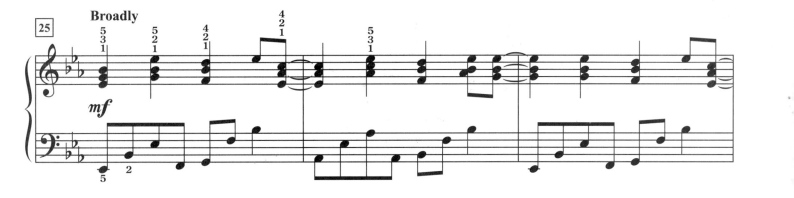

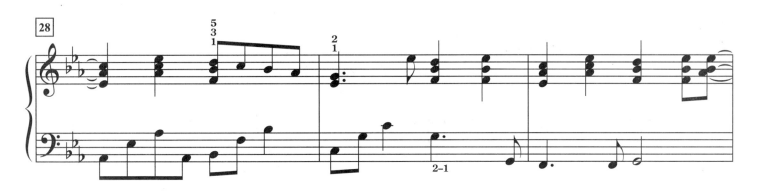

(Approx. Performance Time – 2:30)

Let It Rise

Words and Music by Holland Davis
Arr. Carol Tornquist

(Approx. Performance Time – 3:30)

Mighty to Save

Words and Music by
Reuben Morgan and Ben Fielding
Arr. Carol Tornquist

(Approx. Performance Time – 2:30)

No Other Name

Words and Music by Robert Gay
Arr. Carol Tornquist

(Approx. Performance Time – 3:15)

Oceans
(Where Feet May Fail)

Words and Music by Joel Houston,
Matt Crocker and Salomon Ligthelm
Arr. Carol Tornquist

Slowly (♩ = 72)

(Approx. Performance Time – 3:15)

One Thing Remains
(Your Love Never Fails)

Words and Music by Jeremy Riddle,
Brian Johnson and Christa Black
Arr. Carol Tornquist

(Approx. Performance Time – 2:45)

Open the Eyes of My Heart

Words and Music by Paul Baloche
Arr. Carol Tornquist

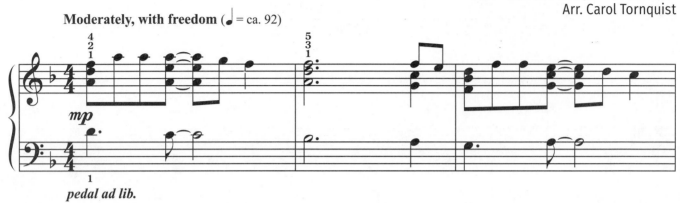

(Approx. Performance Time – 3:00)

Our God

Words and Music by Jesse Reeves,
Chris Tomlin, Matt Redman and Jonas Myrin
Arr. Carol Tornquist

(Approx. Performance Time – 2:45)

The Power of the Cross
(Oh, to See the Dawn)

Words and Music by
Keith Getty and Stuart Townend
Arr. Carol Tornquist

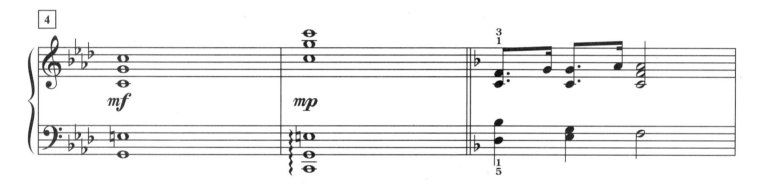

(Approx. Performance Time – 3:15)

Revelation Song

Words and Music by Jennie Lee Riddle
Arr. Carol Tornquist

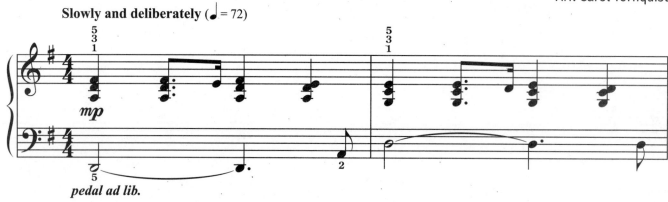

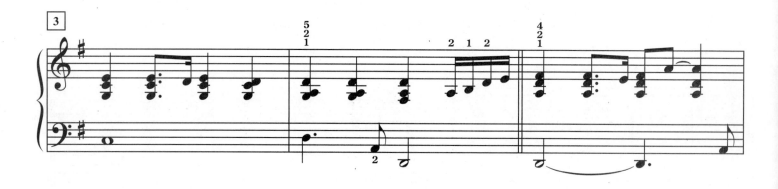

(Approx. Performance Time – 2:15)

There Is a Redeemer

Words and Music by Melody Green
Arr. Carol Tornquist

(Approx. Performance Time – 3:00)

There Is None Like You

Words and Music by Lenny LeBlanc
Arr. Carol Tornquist

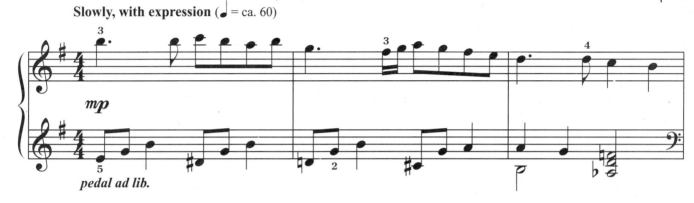

(Approx. Performance Time – 2:45)

This Is Amazing Grace

Words and Music by Josh Farro,
Jeremy Riddle and Phil Wickham
Arr. Carol Tornquist

(Approx. Performance Time – 1:45)

Untitled Hymn
(Come to Jesus)

Words and Music by Chris Rice
Arr. Carol Tornquist

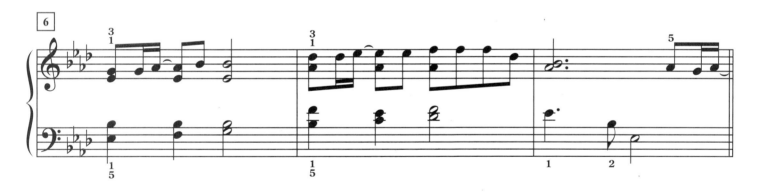

(Approx. Performance Time – 2:45)

We Believe

Words and Music by Matthew Hooper,
Richie Fike and Travis Ryan
Arr. Carol Tornquist

(Approx. Performance Time – 2:30)

Your Grace Is Enough

Words and Music by Matt Maher
Arr. Carol Tornquist

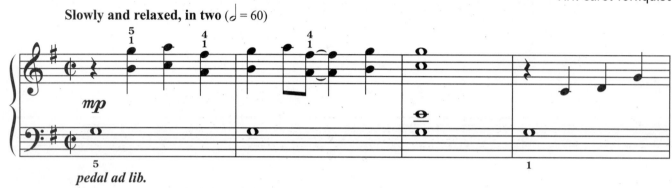

(Approx. Performance Time – 3:30)

Victor's Crown

Words and Music by Darlene Zschech,
Israel Houghton and Kari Jobe
Arr. Carol Tornquist